Learn Your ABC's God's Way

Text Copyright: 1991 Lois Banks
Illustration Copyright: 2006 Lois Banks

Published By:

Uniquely Reading Publishing
19751 Mark, Twain
Detroit, Michigan 48235 USA
Telephone: 1-(877) 863-8190 or (313) 863-8190

All rights reserved. No part of this book may be reproduced in any form without the written permission from Lois Banks.

Author: Lois Banks
Illustrator: Hazel Mitchell
Editor: Lois Banks

Children's Picture Book (age 2-8)

Summary: This unique children's book encourages every child to be kind towards other children and not to hate others for their cultural or religious differences. The message that the Father God gave through His Son Jesus, is a message of love and forgiveness to mankind. This book also encourages children to have a relationship with the Father God daily by accepting His Son Jesus into their heart and life for answers to prayer and success in life.

ISBN: 1-933556-24-2 Soft Cover Edition, 6x9, Perfect Bound, Glossy Finish.

To purchase this book and other products visit
www.uniquelyreading.com

Printed in the United States Of America

Dedication

This book is one of a series that the author intends to publish.

The author hopes that this book will encourage children to always walk with God.

Last but not least, the author would like to dedicate this book to her children Charlton, Candace, Michael and Ashley.

Don't forget the teachings of the word of God.

Love Always,
Mom

Learn your ABC'S God's Way

Written by Lois Banks
Illustrated by Hazel Mitchell

Aa

Read your Bible or Torah all the time.

Bb

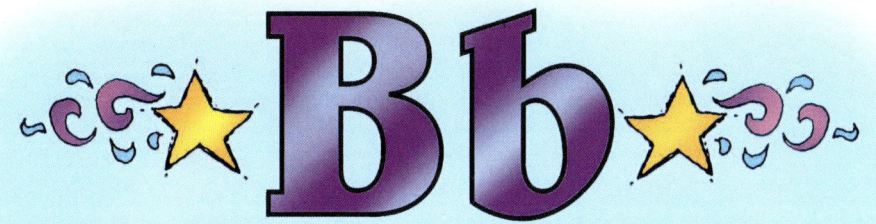

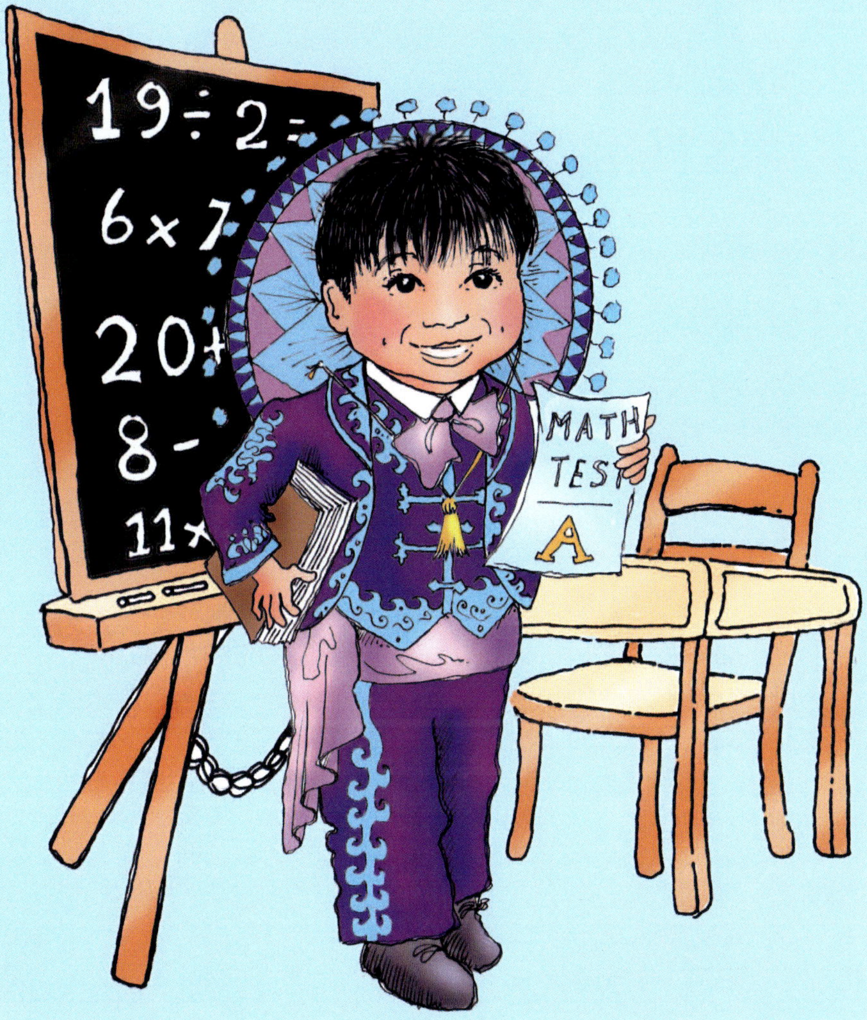

Believe in God, all things are possible.

Count your blessings, you have a lot to be thankful for.

Dd

Don't forget to say your prayers!

Ee

Every time you wake up, be sure to say your prayers.

Find a quiet place and pray to God.

Great is the Lord and greatly to be praised!

God is very powerful,
His powers have no limit.

Always make a joyful noise unto the Lord.

Kk

Keep the word of the Lord inside your heart, so that you can please Him.

Ll

Learn as many of the Holy Scriptures as you can and ask God to help you live a holy life.

Mm

Mary and Joseph are the parents of Baby Jesus.

Nn

Nothing can separate us from the love of God.

Open your heart and share God's love with others.

Sing praises to God, He loves praises!

The word of God is quick and more powerful than a two-edged sword.

Reach for your dreams and God will help your dreams come true.

Sing praises to God; He dwells in the midst of praises!

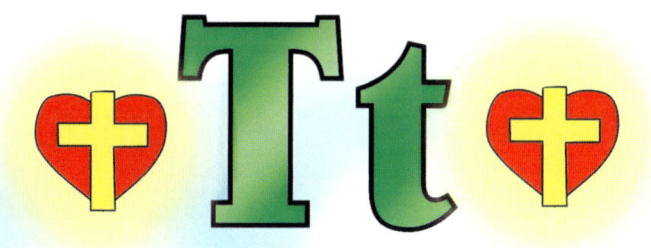

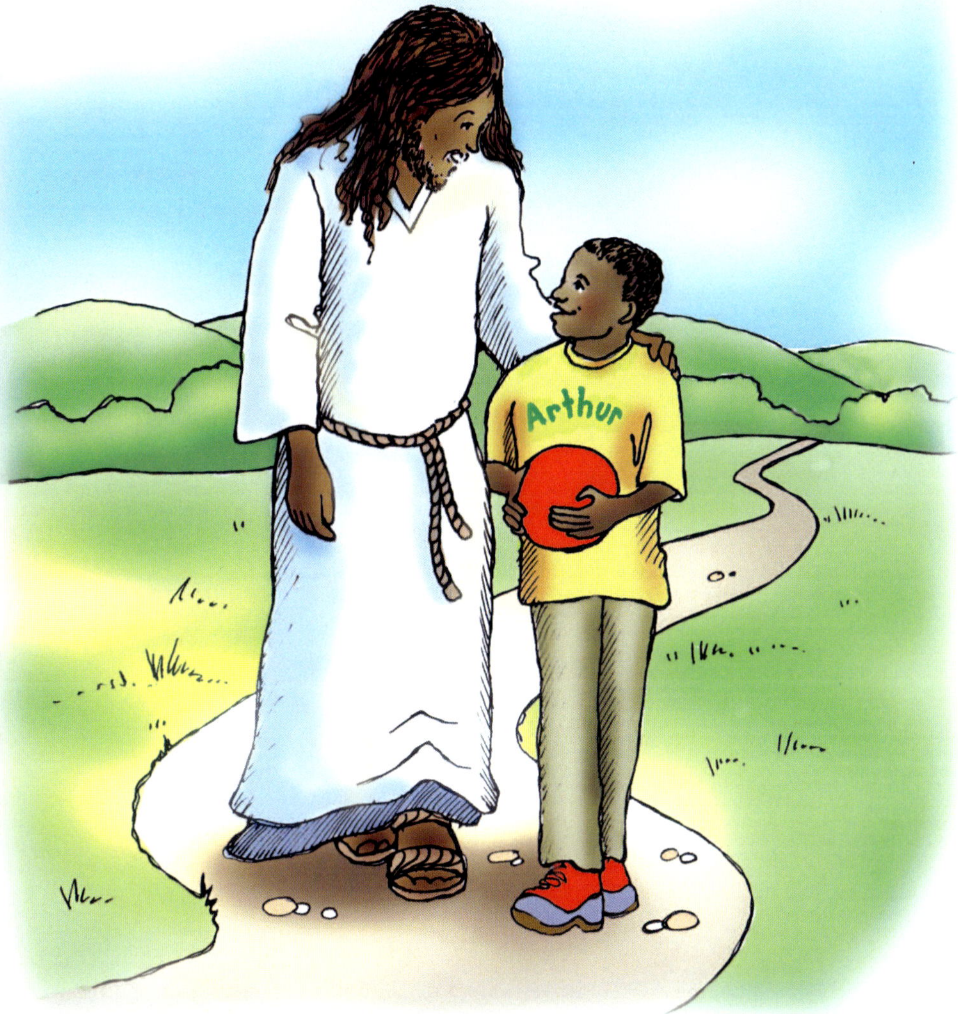

Trust in God, with all your heart.

U u

Use quality time when praying to God.

Vv

View television shows that are only good for you.

With God, all things are possible.

Xx

Always pray extra prayers for people all over the world.

God loves you!

Zebras are just one of the many animals God has created.

Children's Prayer

*Dear Jesus,
Come into my heart
and live.
I believe
that you are
the Son of God.
Amen.*

Lois Michelle Banks was born and raised in Columbus, Ohio. She later moved to Detroit, Michigan and graduated from J.T.P.A. School of Practical Nursing in 1994.

Lois Michelle Banks currently serves God as a practical nurse in the areas of nutritional information to churches and her community and provides nursing skills to the elderly. She also serves God through her company Uniquely Reading Publishing, in which Christian books and products for children and adults are created.

To have Lois Banks as a speaker at your church or special event contact Uniquely Reading Publishing, 313-863-8190 or loisbanks@uniquelyreading.com.

 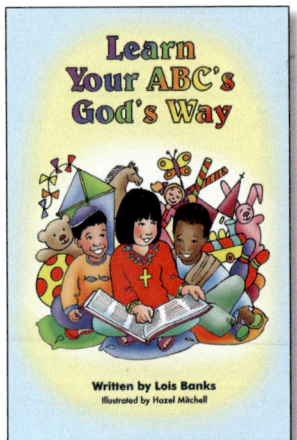 

For more information about our books
and products
or to have Lois Banks
speak at your church or special event
visit us at
www.uniquelyreading.com
or
contact us at
Uniquely Reading Publishing
(313) 863-8190
or
1 (877) 863-8190

19751 Mark Twain
Detroit, MI 48235